TO THE
GODDESSES
AND THE GODS

TO THE GODDESSES AND THE GODS

Poems

TODD JACKSON

Todd Jackson Poetry Las Vegas, Nevada

Contents

Invocation

Musai,

that with each line of these words crushed-
rock dust is cracked and planed down hard upon the consonants,
whereas the finest dust, the lighter-than-air,

it flows throughout the vowels,
it swirls a slow smoke loop or two inside the hollow of an *o* or an *a*
and then released, and away...

Protection. Hestia.

Four snug studio walls.
They absorb the single candle-heat,
and I, cupped within.
I feel the walls glowing through the dark.
I hear, muffled, the hail and the rain
that do not touch me.

This.

It will suffice.

Here.

The Goddess.

Protection.

Hestia.

End of Night

This time, above others, is Apollo's:
Ancient Night has stretched long,
like the North winter stretches long.
There is a blur of purple at the black horizon.
In moments it is spread to a violet efflorescence in the Sky, but
It has not yet rested upon the tree-tops.
The dew still buds, unmelted.
The road is swallowed in the dark.
The crows are awake, and shouting.

Rainbow Boulevard,
Aphrodite

Even in my rear-view mirror, She dances.
White cloud stalks across the country.
It is but my Eyes that cannot discern their motion.
White cloud hovers above the mountains.
In my rear-view mirror I
See the slant where the sunshine stops upon the mountain.
Above this line is grey shadow cast by the white cloudmass
    overhead. Below,
The broad rock shines out beneath,
A cascade of blood red and metal brown.
The cold stone above the slanted line swells
    and gathers within the shadow.
It would be more ancient than the bright rock beneath.
The line would press the bright rock down upon the flat land,
And the rock gleams redder yet for being pinned.
In the vast blue overhead the white clouds
    take the brunt of Sunshine. Their soft fringes blaze gold.
They are the daimones of Apollo,
Who stirs the high thin air with His radiance
To set motion to the world.
Hers, the grace between two dancers.
Cloud and close behind it shadow of cloud
    glide across the desert floor.

And now the slanted line is drawn upward
        as the cloudmass rolls northeast;
As it rises, the mountain is slowly bared in light.

I am held.
On orange and yellow sheets I write your praises on the dashboard.
Cloudburst. My car is open. Cold rare water, now steadier,
And the scent of sudden desert rain.
The raincloud quickly yields to the reasserted shining of the Sun.
The asphalt is licked a proud slate blue,
And all about me,
The red cars' redness stands emboldened.

Misterion

What, then, one man? Though delightful to
Trail the goddess' swath through the wheat
Who there flickers at her heels?
I step into the open.
What am I, upon whom a god shines?
I am catalyzed
As the quartz crust of the bombing range.
Toward what substance?

The City Is Yet Small Before Poseidon

The city is yet small before Poseidon.
Find him in the brown February,
Vegas thick and wet from downpours.
Beneath low-slung ceiling
The land in turn gone brown from rain;
Nor just the scattered matte -turf weed and long grasses,
But tree-stump posts, too,
Soaked, umber,
And flat black puddles in the mudfield
Are a glass to drifting clouds above.
Brown, the little pits in weathered grouting
Between broad grey bricks of wall.
This earth must be damp a good forty feet down.
Over the wall, the horses, sienna,
Bold knight-pieces along the angle of the grey wall,
They bring red flashes inside the brown.
And so too this one red row of bricks,
Slim along the inside angle of the grey wall,
And the power of the horses is the power of forty foot deep of earth
Reared up on hooves.

Lyric

I'd been quite well, alone.
Not that bewildered sort, who scrambles for Some god, any god. Nor
One of those seeking peace of mind. Tho I may have sought war.
I did not need to outlive my death,
Nor now expect to do so,
Though the door, ostensibly, is open.

Kore, Tonight As Though The Night After

Friday night near mid night.

The Moon is a white apple slice Set on one round buttock
And swallowed.

One teardrop's distance down A ruby chip,
A single pin-prick, Mars.

Then yet one more tear's drop Till the grounding line.
Till the first of thorns.

I, Too, Have Been Lame, Hephaistos.

I, too, have been lame, Hephaistos.
I have known the crutches and the wheels.
I hope you never had to make the midnight crawl
on hands and knees and quick,
but I never got grabbed by the bent leg
and flung out off a mountainside.

Hephaistos who knows the pains.

Hephaistos strong and squat and every inch God.
Hephaistos, cuckold who wild-
caught Ares and Aphrodite in the act.
To you the slow resurfacing of the Earth,
that feeds the soil.
Within, hot rock milk rises rounds and sinks in mighty gyres.
It scrapes the mountains of the Core.

Metals bleed out the rock then bleed out one another,
Bucketed deep in black stone hollows,
Red white bright gold slow bubbles rise and pop like frog eyelids.

Heavy hot red lava pools alert to your magic,
it twitches at the wand's touch,
hot pools herald to the next handheld thing dredged up charmed,
and upon which some unwrit legend turns.

Hephaistos the God whose gift is near.

A blade edge peeks through spring green leaves.
The promise of a hand grip fit to mine.
This was made for me.
I had been a man but now I will be something more.
I reach in take hold, I sheathe the prosthetic sublime.

Hephaistos by whom the monster I had feared fears me.

His

is all progression,
the sharpening of predator upon prey,
in Athena's fluid interplay of offense,
defense,
His, the honing of lizard into hawk.

Iatromantis

Shaman, wings yet moist with egg-white, groping shyly
Through the fog whose dampness beads between white feathers,
Vapored slowly through the humid wee-hours.
Proto-dactyl hatched, hollow wing-bones slowly stiffen.
Muscles thickened up upon back-bones
Bunch, and start the wings to heave in grey mist.
Aloft air born. He has shed loose body from body.

Long Beach, Hekate

Under dark She rolls the waves.
She is phosphorus curled inside the wave
That has caught light off the pier's lights that shine downshore.
The waves' skin grey-black from the sea-floor's soot,
And above,
Grey-black from the clouded Night.
The Night-clouds that mass and ripple, Hers,
No less, the phosphorescent smear,
Glowing,
Curled inside the grey-black wave.

Apollonai

I.
The moment that you die shall be Selected
As, among brown boughs, Demeter awaits the white peaches.

II.
An intelligence twitches in the wolflight.
Listen for its quiet stepping as, ahead,
They cross the path,
And when they circle on both sides, gliding through the dark brush,
The quickness of bright eyes.
They have come to teach.
That it is bad to have become infirm.
That one had best keep pace.

III.
There are old things that are of Apollo.
You, the herdsman, you, the wolf.
Thou art the taut predation of the wolves, tuned to human favor.
See. He has gripped hold the horizon with both strong hands,
And dragged it back a great distance,

To where only those whose sight is sharp might see
Birds, like fine specks, wheeling high above the carcass of the Dragon.

See. He has lifted Himself to a perch below the blue sky's midpoint,
Close above the plain. The birds are now scattered, and,
Shining hard upon the new land,
He has left the soil crisp for our footprints.

Long Beach, Aphrodite

.

I am anxious, Lady,
to splash again into the dustbrown surf,
then lay one rose.

Phoebus In Night Air, Chicagoland

Today it came down such that the gray rainwater
    had a silver gleam to it, like curved metal.
The street's black asphalt was swallowed up under
    swirling gray water.
The street was just a broad shape in that water, stretched east-west
between obscure trapezoidal outlines made by the tips of the grass.
The street was made broader by the width of both sidewalks,
both flooded under, the gray water risen above their helpless gutters.
We were all in with the animals, calmer than they,
but concerned about the windows.
Rain blasted the roof. It made a thrilling roar.
It had been a storm that afterward had me tuning in the Weather
    to see what had been destroyed,
And indeed three trees had blown down just on this street,
Two of these, crashed on houses.
I'd forgotten about the trees.
At the corner, at the new house, both an ambulance and
    a fire-truck are parked in the driveway.
Now it is afterward, and the air is stopped with humidity.
Now it is One AM in Chicagoland, middle-time America,
    near the center of the four-spread hand of the American hours.

The rain blast has scared the mosquitoes clear out of the night,
and there are fireflies here grounded on the concrete, as if dying.
The tall young trees bend down their branches,
        springing with leaves, flush upon the roof.
The air is humid to where it seems a particulate gray-black mist.
        It is night.
A couple yards forward is a low stone wall, describing the limit
        of this concrete backyard court where I sit and smoke,
And beyond it, the backyard proper, several trees, and both the grass
        and the black tree bark are glutted with rain.

And well behind the stone wall, the fence, straight wood posts nailed
        tight together along two crossing beams.

Night, but suburban night;
it is not, then, the utter western blackness of One AM
        in the hours west of Chicagoland's hour,
the blackness of the cornfields, and of the open desert.
Rather, the suburban night,
        the great bright Chicago just past the horizon,
        as if its spires might still prick up above the arc of the Earth.
Their brilliance, huddling west of the black Lake,
        defying nightfall just as surely as their sheer ascent
        defies the gravity of the Earth.
Even here, almost an hour south,
        there are the burglar lights of neighbors' houses,
        and the piercing white headlights of a passing car.

It is not nature. It is the legacy of human brilliance against nature.
It is the straightness of the human back.
This light is collectively faint,
but it has been as if cider-pressed through the mist,
and it has blossomed out into the black night
        like a bright blood cloud spreading beneath a surface of water,

and so this blackness is electric lit, alert and gleaming. And more.
I can just make out an uncertain greenness in the gray leaves
        that lean down above.
It is a green so dim that it seems imagined.
Apollo he is all sublimed inside this suburban night.
A gold river of light flows through a break in the trees.
        It is almost tactile, a plasma,
        its source is Sunlight off the cloud-shrouded Moon.
Its riverbanks, marking the river from the night, are sharply lined.
Light flows over the stone wall and spills down
        into the wet concrete court, pooling.

This light is aeons older than humankind,
        first hatched aeons past in the heart of the Sun. It is old,
        like rock is old.
In the night mist this old mighty light
        is mixed through and through with
the electric lit skyline of Chicago, hatched in the human mind,
And He, being either;
I have learned
That to see these lights as One light
Is to glimpse the shining off His arrows,
Invincible as the break of morning.

Hymn to the Goddess Night

Nyx,
In bedded in each of objects,
Enfolding all.
Hers the black palms, that swim the void,
From which each that is
Must receive permission.

Hermes

October before the clock-shift, Sundown,
And the remainder of the Sun is the white-shock dazzling
Cracked across the long black claw of the mountain line.
Inside are the coins, copper and copper in-lined in silver,
Piled in corners swept of dust.
They will stand watch.
They will hold the Sun-frost into night.
They will protect the child.

Aphrodite, Just Off Flamingo Road

Three-quarters of the glass vial
From the Hindu smoke shop,
good tight string work sounding in the air.
Of the vial, Black Orchid,
I put flame to the oil, then shut the windows.
The ceiling fan blades whip round,
The blades carve a circle in the popcorn ceiling.
Aphrodite has scented the oil.
She smiles a rainbow underside the ceiling,
An arc, as bow shock off the arc the blades have dug.
The rainbow shows two quick colors,
And the first is something in the violets
Inside which, red swells embryonic.
Then just a quick swoop of the red,
A skimming along the inside arc of violets,
And inside that. To yellow
Till all surrender to the great broad of green,
That at last dissolves into the sizzling white sunlight
Blast through the sluice of window-blinds.
Here, along this little patch of ceiling, She smiles.

Now is tomorrow, the cinnamon stick smeared with the sweet oil,
Tall among the abundant leaf.
Aphrodite's, the power that binds the leaf.
It is put to flame, it is passed between worlds.
She has scented the potpourri.
Her soft palms burst into flowers.
I will draw open the window-blinds, and open the windows

Our Sun, Too, Is The
Iron Sun

Our Sun, too, is the iron Sun.
Aetna here flares down.
Apollo's, the razor inside the Sun, that cuts.
This Sun promises time is short.

Before this Sun you will know yourself.

Hymn to Hades

Hades, in Whom I shall be silent.
Hades, in Whom I shall be still.
This old pain I've feared will never end

Will.

Persephone

That very morning she had stood before them.
She spoke straight and true as a Goddess.

"O my people do not fear.
There is a crown beneath the grass. It will be mine
And I will rescue all of mortal kind that eats my Mother's grain.

"O my people do not fear.
There is a power beneath the grass. It will be mine
And I will hollow world after world from out the dark.

"There you may rest.
There you may ready yourself for the new birth.

"O my people do not fear.
When next the Lord comes riding
I will be the girl with flowers in her hair.
Neither will my fingers tremble as I pin them there."

A Piety

I had been satisfied.
The dead surrendered to the winds,
I praised the God they too had praised
As though those long consecrated to the pyres,
Then raised Moonward as ash
Had by now filtered above the cirrus clouds
And left the blue sky clean beneath them.

They were neither my nation nor my blood. I would breathe,
And imagine I did not draw them in with every breath.
I would stand here,
In the audacious city blooming off the desert floor
Honoring the sacred gulf between myself
        and He who stands astride the broad-faced mountain
Soaring to a peak, tallest among the western ridge
And crossed daily by the ascending slash of the Sun.

But I would have that space cleared
Of those who once too stood apart this distance
And shouted Ie! Ie Paian!
East, the angeloi rise to greet the morning.

East, opposite Apollo's mountain
A package of F-16s appears above me, and is gone.
First one, then a pause, and another,

Four grey shafts upon the blue,
Streaking west toward the mountain.
Then the lead rolls right, metal wing dipped,
and One by one, the fighters vanish northwest.
Only now, the engine shriek ebbed off,
The alerted wailings of all the car alarms.

Come dusk, they will return in tight couples.
I peer into a black nozzle and regard the gold jet-wash,
Kindled, now kindled low
Which only minutes ago had shot back a hard Mach diamond,
The fighter craft a faint streak then in the high thin air.
I witness this and am satisfied among the living.
I do not pine for the curvèd prows of Salamis
Nor the crewmen, each long taken up into Night.

Here is good country, in a good world,
And the Gods are with us.
They are proved *athanatoi*, the Deathless Ones.
I have disremembered the moment,

But that it came in a single moment
Is printed on my mind.
It came like a footstep across an unmarked line.
I have learned to see in just this tracklessness
The tracks of Gods.

It came, and afterward I heard a hollow pit inside the air
That once was thick with the hymns as though with moisture.
Each year brought the choirs to Claros. They
Marched singing through the triple gate.
They sang before their fathers, who themselves had sung.
The priest had sipped of the water, and was ready.

Mnêsomai oude lathômai Apollônos hekatoio, honte theoi kata dôma
Dios tromeousin ionta...

They sang a thousand years, and then cut short.
The words remain as fishbones in the sand.
The music is devoured as mortal flesh is devoured.
What came and was passed to me was no enthusiasm,
But an overhearing of the God's heart,
Cast upon lost honors, and an ancient friendship.
Afterward, then, my own choice
To give the old words voice, and lay them upon my altar.
Let them gather in the air with the white incense smoke,
Above the pure water and the candle flames.

Delian, bless this speaking before the candle flames.

enth' ek nêos orouse anax hekaergos Apollôn,
asteri eidomenos mesôi êmati: tou d' apo pollai

I give voice, who have no more faced a vowel tripthong
Than the walls of Ilium.
Still a beauty rises off this speaking,
Beautiful the way this Sun-blast desert, where a constant
Purple blush descends from the dawn air to
Rest upon the salmon roofing tiles and upon the desert
Crust also is beautiful.
The stormcloud sage will make these words a fine familiar.
A lone stealth fighter drifts low above our roofs.
Slow, and otherworldly,
It is itself the shadow it would cast.
Alone, and it does not break northwest but glides due west
Toward the mountain.
I am ready.
I will press these old words

Till they are ground again to song.
Afterward, Apollo, only you know what magic.

Interrogation In Ice and Silver

Best read with champagne.

.

Not Delphi, that survives,
Where again, furtively, wild flowers are laid on white stones,
But here, round the spaceward face of Earth.
Night is drawn across, but the Sun is dug into the rock
And the city pavement is humming.

The Moon light is fitted tight upon the Moon disc.
There we have set down track,
Where Hekate gathers her daimones, who make no track.
We have stood atop the clean white mountains,
Reviewed the winding of world about world. There,
There is not city.
Only the marks, from the men's boots,
Spread random into the fines.
They are not yet script.

Here, Las Vegas,
The city is lights sprinkled across the desert floor.

I stand at angle to the Earth,
Review the winding of world about world.
The black robe has swallowed the mountains.
Left awake the sweep of her hem, the glittering in the dust,

Left to her daughter's care.
I have sifted quarters out black soot made soil
From the burnings.

Two palmsful of the silver discs, bent and twisted, un stamped.
A wind-whorl now, cupped in my ear,
The whistling, and then the voice within the whistling:

Be alert, as the serpent that has heard the bow snap.
You will perceive the Sun God's hand upon the Moon,
You will refine the Sun shine upon the Moon
        from within the Moonlight.
Then the voice in the whistling is vanished in the whistling.

Time has come. Around the world,
Eos' whole palm now is flat upon the white marble.
Apollon has cracked the horizon line.

Here dark is shattered by candlelight.
Speak, put flame to the leaves,
Speak, set the Hymn airborne,
Sit, alert,
As she has whispered.
I am still.
Alert, my curved back-bone straight,
And peeled, this body, to precede the bodies.

Moon concave Mojave.
Desert facing desert across the black channel
    that is choked with light.
The Moon pulls under the desert floor,
to the hollows that once were packed with silver.

There we dug the silver out the ground. Here we sucked the water.
We take up the silver and we churn it into lights.
We are here because the old place got old, and we didn't.
There are not lights in your city as in my city.

We have the lights. Bring silver.
We have the silver. Send water.
So lives the city.

I cut ground.
Wet crust at a shopping center site
Hacked a trough diagonal across a lane
Then set to break the trough deep for the pipe.
One pipe for the lights, and one for the water.
I was sore that night.
So lives the city.
The concrete shell is open to the wind.
Here we have willed the city.
We will the city in the churning of the lights.

Some times the Earth dreams of all our dying. She waits,
She who will take the cities down, But not my city.

I get four feet.
I watch the Sun shine down the crack I dug.
Here is the last place left for cities.
There is no mercy in this crust for the pick.

A mood descends. In,
Four thousand some miles, the center.
I get four feet cut before the Sun glides through the lateral.
One little nick across the thick lateral.
The Earth is hard below the lateral.
She takes down the animal. She keeps the bone.
She grinds me down at the ankle, at the knee.
Lives whisper upon the Earth,
Deflect up off, and scatter in the dust-whorl above the lateral.
She, who is real. In,
Four thousand miles, the center of the real.
Iron is crushed to juice.
The iron churns, and is still.

I circle the iron, that will break me down upon the crust.
The wind is empty across the desert, and whispers Vanity.
But now I have heard another Goddess inside the breeze,
        who whispers secrets,
And mine is the vainest city.

Moon concave Mojave.
Desert facing desert across the black channel that is
        choked with light.
Whereas,
one-third round the Earth,
Abroad first continent and then the least of two great oceans,
Through the pinch of the dawn-splashed sea, that broke massed rock,
As, west, Sun has cracked the horizon line,
Then up the north mountains, where the God speaks cities.

The winds are electric from the black robe just swept east.
Prayers inside the air entwine with the high wind,
Conspire an airborne village overhead the north mountains.

Prayers bask in bright cool Sunlight.
They shout Paean upon the mountain.

They splash his name upon the waters.

En pontôi d' eporouse demas delphini

Up, from among ripe flesh lightning through the blue wave,
Up, and upon the sea-borne men attendant the black ship,

Each man bred on still bright dolphins studded in blue frescoes,
    as at Knossos.
No catch like this. A God has splashed aboard, who stills men.
It is Apollon, who knows the number of the sands.
Apollon the line between the stone set, and the stone to be set.
Apollon every Sun and all Suns, frosting in the Robe's black fur,
    pooled in One,
He stands aboard.

We, who know the shores.
We, toward whose homeland men will whisper, Atlantis. We listen.
I don't yet envision the life made on this mountain,
But the God chooses well, who chose us.

Another will come, from the country.
Hers, to churn Word into word inside her body
As the God speaks cities.
Ours to sit rapt, who know the shores.
Disembarked, the anchor cracked through the blue water,
Then down,
The ship held still on the water's pane. Below,

The dolphin loll about the rope.
The Sun is in the water, and carresses them.

The dolphin swim through hoops of Sunshine that
     stroke their bodies.
To this spot the people will come, zigzag through the mountain.
The God will send them straight.
They will troop back down to their ships,
anchored in the bay as our ship now is anchored in the bay.

The dolphin squeal forth into the water,
Sonar waves fan out broad, above Sun-shot crabs and starfish,
     across seafloor,
Ahead, to seek Poseidon's favor.
The dolphin squeal, that will escort the black ships sent forth
     to found the city,
Ripe flesh lightning through the bluewhite wave.
Apollon will speak Siracusa, whose bay will drown an empire.
He will speak Cyrene, that will breed Kallimachus,

H'oion ho t'opollonos

Speak Elea, that will breed Parmenides,
     and the city underground Elea,
That will be hacked out the land, and covered.
Speak Kroton and the town that will blow out off Kroton,
     like a bright soap bubble,
Wherein Pythagoras will slow churn the people into angels.
Speak Naxos, that will send the Sphinxes.

Speak Marseilles, whose name will slip from tongue to tongue,
     but remain one singing.
Speak not the city, Sparta, but the Law that will set the city,
To be held in mind, then spoken, and not writ down.
Speak Messina Sybaris, Megara Hyblaia
     and then Selinas, Cumae and Cadmeia, Ciris, Gela,
They will sacrifice to you,

God who led them, straightaway on the sand.

Good earth, near those beaches, and good water.
Sail out very much further, and then start walking.
You can see the Earth curving down.
The Earth will curve, and close,
  and now I am in the last place left for cities,
Above tough dry earth getting dryer.

Full Moon.
She has snowed a powder silver down superfine upon us,
Upon the long top curve of the white wood fencing beams,
Silver superfine upon the boy who picks nuggets off the roadside.
Moon powder glows white blue white in the leaping dog's fur.
We shall revise the center of the real.
What was near four thousand miles underfoot, reset,
  now not less than seven hundred feet
Overhead, and in open air.
The stars sigh. We are to people the Night.
Ice clouds await us in the Night.
One day Las Vegas will scale the shaft of light.
Then, the stone set, and the stone to be set.
Staid freedom. As I have stood.
Our children will watch the wind grind these mountains down,
One grain after another.

Theirs...

Hekate's Is The Crooked Moon

Cowled,
But loosely so,
So that jewel points bloom out a dark coiffure.

Early March.
Cold rains have crossed California
Then rolled over the Sierras and dipped down upon us,
And six straight days chilled Las Vegas.
These cold rains, then carried East along the high wind,
And did great mischief there;
Snow lies two feet deep and more all up the seaboard.
Back here, back West, the Valley lies refreshed.
At midweek there had been a tight seam of heat inside two cold days,
And Saturday we burst into the seventies.

Tonight, the summit of Mount Charleston,
The high point of Earth in this broad County;
The crooked Moon hangs above, just off the peak of black Night.
Hekate's, the crooked Moon, that slices even Night.
The Moon is framed, off-center,
        by the silhouetted tips of the bristlecone pines,

That sprouted when quick girls still dared bulls at Minos.
No longer even a green blush now within that soft mass;
The pines are but blacker shapes against black Night,
Jagged in the corners of my sight, the stars all hid behind.
While, below, warm spring sunlight has stroked Las Vegas,
Then soothed it with cool winds.
It is white winter here atop Mount Charleston,
Where the cloudwater fell as it would fall two thousand miles east,
As snow.

Winter had entered the valley as a nymph in white taffetta,
Billowing through Night;
She drifted southeast, sailing among the clouds,
Snagged underneath by the tips of all the Sierras,
And above,
Snagged also upon the crooked Moon;
The winter nymph here has paid due tribute
To Hekate,
Then flowed eastward in a shredded gown.
Mount Charleston, as the tall peak,
        has snagged its own big patch off the gown,
And I am standing here, the black man among two amid white snow,
        and the dogs.
Here, cast against white snow, as
Above, on white moondust.
I look now with all my eyes
And behold, the splash of dogprints in the snow.

Io Hekate who knows the third road. Io Hekate who holds the key.
For the Moon, and Nevada,
        are two great concaves toward each other,
Split by black broad space
As great palms outspread in the Night,
So that the Moon, and Nevada, are not aimless wanderers;

They are pinned,
Such that that tight cislunar space has sprung five whirlpools,
And close upon Nevada, encircling the Earth,
        a skin of gathered Sunfire.
I leave bootprints in the snow atop the mountain, as
Above, in that white sliver dangled before distant stars
There are boot prints studded in the Moon dust.

Io Hekate,
Who knows the steep way.
Io Hekate who holds the key.

Hers is the Moon, and the crooked Moon.
Hers that part of Dionysos' sap that poisons and heals.
Hers is the jellyfish sting.
And that bright droplet off the rattler's fang,
That inside itself is whirling as it dangles there.
Hers, the thirst for riches, that gives focus to Spirit,
And the thirst for revolution, that gives focus to Soul.
Hers, the hymen between salesman and closer,
And the big red X on the board.
Hers, the black and the red of the dice. Hers, the garlic bulb,
That is poison unto poison itself, and thereby heals.
Hers, my recent trade of blood against poverty,
And that blood pays cheap.
Hers the nuggets still dug deep in the land, unpicked, Waiting,
And the black oil that is the pressed rot of ancient flesh,
And that pools and surges within the Earth,
Then sails the broad seas in ships more numerous
Than breadcrumbs strewn before an audience of birds,
And all, because it burns.
Hers the honorific, *Nigger,* that is the curse,
        and delight, of my people,
The choice of Black, and the weight inside that choice,

That may not now be unchosen.
For we now are Hers, And Her grip will not be broken.
Hers the dark shining in the abyss,

Earth's bowels burst hot through the ocean floor,
Hers the weird dark forests that thrive there,
In the pressure.
Hers the ice and the metal in the Moon.
Hid beneath deep rock, yet there is no hiding
From the torchlight.
Hers, the quarter million miles of cold death.
Hers is that knowing of woman that woman may only know
By knowing herself, and among the herbs.
Hers, the mystique of woman.

I know a lady, skin the color of moonlight on bundled wood.
People are dying in her dreams who aren't dead yet.
That comes afterward, and soon.

Under Night,
Winding down the mountain road.
My friend and I observe upon the city, art, and blackjack. She
I cannot long speak of. She
Is not yet fully speakable in this time.
But down in that great splash of lights below,
Mine is not the only candle lit
For Hekate. Yes,
Were She to, with a wave of Her hand,
Snuff the brilliant plumage of the Strip,
And Downtown's yellow-red-white gleaming,

Were She then to shut down the straggler lights of Summerlin,
Of North Las Vegas,
And leave only candles lit for Gods

The valley floor would at first lie black as the ring of mountains
Before Apollo brings them forth with the morning.
The valley floor would at first lie black,
But in time the eyes would focus, and soon make out
Pricks of light, only several, but definite.
Scattered, and yet a gathering,
Witness to the returning of the time.

It is growing warmer down the slope.
We descend from winter toward spring.
But now two fingers on my right hand are struck cold.
Cold has climbed up my knuckles,
Till , taking fingernail to lips, I find it ice.
I remind myself of my good health overall,
Yet can not not ask, Which does this mean? Stroke or heart attack?

No. It is that She has taken my hand.
She who comes and goes in dread.
I am honored. I will choose some fine thing tomorrow
To set before the purple candle.
Io Hekate who sees the shape.
Io Hekate who sees the key.

Hekate's is the crooked Moon
Unto its final silver pinch
Descending dark.

Hymn to Orpheus

Orpheus, I honor you.
Remind me that to keep the Lyre before me
Is to walk from world to world tuned in
To the table-talk of the Gods.

Let Sunlight come to me through the skein of music.
Let the Earth's colors be harmonized
Even as they splash at random across the grass.

Keep me student to the therapies that ease the heart
And, lyre in hand, first step followed by second step by third,
Remind me not to turn around.

Hera, Singly

I.

It is proposed
That once were only little tribes of us,
and scattered, and hunted down by monsters,
and the Gods appeared to peek through a single face,
and God was Hera.

Later poets held those days,
real or misremembered, against you,
upright on their stones in hot slander.
But I know you are merciful,
having let that many die old in bed .

That many, and not one more.
Your mercy had been tempted bad before.

Hera's,
the pride to repay a blow with two,
And should it come down to monsters, then monsters it shall be.

II.

Was the Bride implied within you, even then,
          and from whence, the Groom?

Hera,
Bride and Queen
When such were but a dream.
While you waited,
While Zeus, yet half-titanic,
out screwed the whole tight Cosmos into many.

Teach me the grace to hold a lonely office,
The patience to build this seat
Though I build for others I cannot know.
Teach me how to dine alone in cool elegance.

Lady, narrow the scope of my concern
To this cup, this fork, these candles
So that when the people return
They will find the banquet well-appointed

Though I be long gone into the fine wind, and into winds yet finer.
While, bewitched by you,
all the little curses burst in a hail of flower-petals.

They fall about your feet and sing your praises.

Evanescent Are The Saffron Veils

Captured winds engorge my sails,
Stations dangerously undermanned.
Evanescent are the saffron veils.

Sharing sea-lanes with majestic whales,
Free from priestly reprimand.
Captured winds engorge my sails.

Intuition guides where charting fails.
Voicing praise to Gods from every land.
Evanescent are the saffron veils.

Salted breezes sing exotic tales,
Thirty times retold and each more grand.
Captured winds engorge my sails.

Weighting foreign spice upon the scales.
Flood-tide sweeps my foot-prints from the sand.
Evanescent are the saffron veils.

Scrolls are buried deep within the bales.
Copy quick, this sacred contraband.
Captured winds engorge my sails.
Evanescent are the saffron veils.

Hymn to Apollo

Phoebus Apollo,
Zeus' own Idea of a God
Teach me to discern the light upon the cup
From the cup itself.
Teach me to discern the cup unseen, that sits between all cups,
In stillness, upon the table of Zeus.
Teach me to discern the Flawless that sits
Between all Flawed things.

Hymn to Athena

Ready me, Athena. Stand close and guide.
The seafloor rises as the bow cuts the waves
            into divergent trails of foam.
It is you who search the shoreline in the dark.
Your eyes spot out the dangers hidden in the dark wood.

Guide me, Lady,
To the glory somewhere glittering in the cliff-face.
Breathe upon me,
That my pulse might calm, the procession of my thought, clarify.
Athena, whistle-clean these synapses
Let the electric fire of Zeus speak straight through to every fiber.
Steady me, Goddess, for that that awaits onshore.

Hymn to Hekate Atomos (an invocation)

The Atom is the Crossroads of One and Mind.
The nucleus, Her bitches by Her will confined.
Whirl, Hekate.
Emit the manifold of bodies Then set them all ashine.

You, the first of matter.

You alone, in whom is matter perfect.

You, in whom matter is readied and made proliferate.

Whirl, Hekate.
The Atom is the Crossroads of One and Mind.
The nucleus, Her bitches by Her will confined.

And so another body long ungodded stands assigned.

Prometheus In Seven Lines

Sun unrisen.
A rooster dreams tonight's last dream.
The canyon walls are bouncing wild with shadows.
Overhead, in still, dark outline,
The rock on which I'll pay for all of this in plenty.

All of which begins toward tonight.
Now it's all about this spark so bright.

The Psychic Stowaway

Golden Fleece receding in my thoughts.
Alexandrian and Theurgist,
I inhabit Jason as my sheath.
We, the Goddess-haunted Argonauts.

Cruising speed's about eleven knots.
Colchis' outline sharpens in the mist.
Many dangers led us to this heath.
Golden Fleece receding in my thoughts.

Silken black, with scent of apricots,
One Medea's tress encoiled 'round our wrist.
Hers, to guide this princeling to his wreath.
We, the Goddess-haunted Argonauts.

Undersea, Hecate draws our lots
Wills the rosy-tipping waves to whist.
Hers, the colder steely blue beneath.
Golden Fleece receding in my thoughts.

For Medea's sake the Goddess plots.
Time di-verges at our nuptial kiss.
He returns with bride and sword in fist,
Conquers what his bloodline must bequeath.
He, the first-recruited Argonaut.

I remain, the Princess in my cot.
Soon I take the scent of apricot.
In each other's magic we assist,
Sifting wisdom from reptilian teeth,
Golden Fleece a blanket to our cot.
I, the last-recruited Argonaut.

Hymn to Pythagoras

Pythagoras, Hero,
Teach me to hear the screams
of these upon whom I now dine.

Make of tomorrow's meal,
over whom I will pray,
an ambrosia,

So that in that plate, tomorrow's plate,
I join the Gods at table.

Dionysos, Who Must Be Bound

Dionysos,
who must be bound. Dionysos,
who will split the leather straps.
Soon, Dionysos.

Summer broke in Vegas.
The heat recedes
to the two high late-day hours,
Four o'clock to six,
Pinched between
long cool stretches of dry breeze.
Soon, the season of wine and surrender.

Dionysos,
who must be bound. Dionysos,
who strains the leather straps.
The Sun has ticked autumnal.
Now, Dionysos!

Hymn to Herakles Ouranios
(an invocation)

.

Herakles, twinkling in the Starry Night,
Return, remind me again
That once you slept upon this Earth
That you felt ache, that you bled,
Knew victory and hunger, and finally knew flames.

Come down from red Rasalgethi the Alpha Herculis,
Down from yellow-white Irena.
Down from the double-star Kornephoros.

You who slew the lion and the Hydra and the birds.
You brought up the many-headed dog from Hades' door,
And I've a many-headed dog to drag back down.

Herakles!
You became Stars within the Starry Night.
What, then, shall I become?

Smile upon me as I take up my labors.
Send good word that it is not too late
To have been a Son of Zeus.

For you brought up the many-headed dog from Hades' door,
And I've a many-headed dog to drag back down.

The Serapis Suite (an invocation)

I.

Come, Apollon.

Gather broken Serapis, as

Once you gathered Dionysos,

And proved Him Zagreus evergreen.

Come, Phoebus Apollon,

Let us sing Serapis whole.

And prove the interrupted era, evergreen.

Let Gods dance again

On the tiles of the Serapaion.

Come, Apollon.

Gods are budding in the grain

Sing them high-sprouting,

Sing them back from the Stars.

II.
Hail Serapis for the mysteries in the grain
Packed in a million hulls then scattered across the Sea.
Hail Serapis in whom the Cosmopolis is fed

And who concentrates the grain for the wise.
Hand me the gold-rimmed cup, Lord Serapis,
That I might grow wise.
Hail Serapis, first glimmered in the barley
That rises and sets along the banks
With the rise and set of the River.

III.
AmmonZoonPloutonDionZagreus
AmmonZoonPloutonDionSerapis

Hail, Serapis
Sun that shines Below
You who are Helios Apollon
Relentless glider through the aetherial flesh Of Zeus

Whose wheels mark the Seasons and the Hours
Their bridge to the Timeless
As Being's, to Image. You who are Hades.

Still, as Earth and Heavens wheel about you Serapis
I feel the heat of your flesh
Rising up through the Earth that is your flesh
Rising up through the grass blades.
One Zeus One Hades One Serapis

AmmonZoonPloutonDionZagreus
AmmonZoonPloutonDionSerapis
AmmonZoonPloutonDionZagreus

Serapis.
My heart, that is Still, and that Wheels,
And is One.
AmmonZoonPloutonDionZagreus
AmmonZoonPloutonDionSerapis

IV.
Hail Serapis
The God who was spoken

And spoken by one granted to speak Gods
Basileus, Pharaoah, Soter,
Ptolemy calling out to the people
Ptolemy calling out to Capitols across the sea.
Hail Basileus,
Who recalled the hooves and the hetaroi
Who took the throne of Two Kingdoms
But saw a realm spread wide, an unbounded whole,
And knew its great God
And spoke.
Hail Basileus,
Who perceived the shapes of the God
In the Dawn Sea-mist that sweeps across the Cosmopolis
And spoke the Name.

V.
Serapis of the serpentine Silk Road
Of many tongues and many Kings.
Kings face your coinage, Lord Serapis,
Caesar and Alexandros, Ptolemy and Kanishka,
With your face behind them all,
Guarantor,

Power behind the nations, Serapis seen and unseen.
Patron of adventures Embodied and Disembodied.
Serapis of occult texts
Passed among the peppers and the homespun,
Men whispering behind the caravan,
Passing papyri hid in their sleeves.
Serapis, Guarantor of good things in this world
        and better still in the next.
Watch over me, Lord Serapis. I ride East.

VI.
Praises to Amun
First of the Ennead.
Amun of the Ram's Horn
And the ceaseless inward spiral.
Praises to Amun who is God Zero,
Amun favored of Alexander,
Hidden power, ever-vanishing,
Self-born secret of the One
For whom Plotinus' teacher was named.
Take me, Lord, up-river,
To your sacred precincts.

VII. Grain In Time

Grain in Time is intertwined impressed.
Precedent to Number rose the Grain.
Press the harvest down upon the harvest.

Elders, having won their time of rest
Noted regularity in rain.
Grain in Time is intertwined and pressed.

Stars had captured Flood in their arrest,
Planets planted in elliptic lanes.
Press the harvest down upon the harvest.

Year by year, this thesis met the test:
Winter fields would next year rise and wane.
Grain in Time is intertwined impressed.

They controlled for passing blight or pest,
Recognizing Mind in the refrain,
Press the harvest down upon the harvest.

Here implied, the theory we invest:
This life reaped to spring forth once again.
Grain in Time is intertwined and pressed.
Press the harvest down upon the harvest.

VIII. Let Us Turn Aside This Blackened Bread

Gold that sizzles always turns to lead.
Nymphs let cry among the sycamore:
"Let us turn aside this blackened bread."

Hell Eternal, such a fertile dread.
Whip affrighted masses through the door.
Gold that sizzles always turns to lead.

"For Lorenzo, terrorized abed.
For Hypatia whom they shred to gore.
Let us turn aside this blackened bread.

"Worship they no God but Book instead.
Spirit gleaned from Nature they abhor.
Gold that sizzles always turns to lead.

"For Skythopolis' undried bloodshed.
For the disenchanted Earth they tore.
Let us turn aside this blackened bread.

Gold authentic yields the Golden Thread,
Useless as an instrument of war.
Gold that sizzles always turns to lead.
Let us turn aside this blackened bread."

IX. Hellenistic

Phoebus, dig the new foundations deep,
Golden-tinted towers stroking Space.
Wake Dinocrates, so long asleep.

Through these tower walls no rain will seep.
Strong defenders stand at every face.
Phoebus, dig the new foundations deep.

Haulers hauling silk and cassereep,
Roads upon which multitudes will pace.
Wake Dinocrates, so long asleep.

Voices of the people in our keep,
Each alone to crack this carapace.
Phoebus, dig the new foundations deep.

Here, a soul released will take its leap.
Reborn god, a mortal form unlaced.
Wake Dinocrates, so long asleep.

Sunrise finds no chrysalis to sweep.
Listen for our wings, we've left no trace.
Phoebus, dig the new foundations deep.
Wake Dinocrates, so long asleep.

Apollo: Download While Jaywalking

Communed the God of Lycurgus:

You are not, your self, alone.
You are of a society, in whom your parents met,
As theirs before,
That taught you how to read and how to think,
That will bury your body when you die,
Which won't be long.

Even if another sixty years it won't be long.

It is a good, to walk the law,
Even down to little things,
When you think no one is watching.

Villanelle for the Goddess Hekate

There'll be that of me that yet survives.
Just before I step aboard this barque
Someone slices Soul from Bone with knives.

Through my tissue, cold and moist, it dives.
Sulfur struck upon my spine will spark.
There'll be that of me that yet survives.

As a mass of buzzing stirs in hives
Birdsong lurks implicit in the lark.
Someone slices Soul from Bone with knives.

Watching Intellect She then connives
To imprint on Image Her remarque.
There'll be that of me that yet survives.

She repeats the shape of Mind in countless lives,
Then recalls them to Herself when each goes dark.
Someone slices Soul from Bone with knives.

Sure as Ten's division in two Fives,
Sure as iron dropped on sand will leave its mark,
There'll be that of me that yet survives.
She will slice my Soul from Bone with knives.

Urban's Noir

"This will be the final night of stars.
Curs from Paris to Macau applaud.
Soon the lady dons a dead peignoir.

"Crystalline perfection's avatars,
Shed some grace upon us with a nod.
This will be the final night of stars.

"Snapped between his teeth my Censor's bar.
This is not to say he's been declawed.
Soon the lady dons a dead peignoir.

"Word by now has soaked the seminars,
'Galileo has evicted God!'
This will be the final night of stars.

"Endless tragicomic abattoir,
Soiling her hem with common blood.
Soon the lady dons a dead peignor.

"They'd been Soul's attentive registrars.
Awe one offered them was moral awe.
This will be the final night of stars.
Night the Lady dons a dead peignoir."

Toast to Hades

To You,
Who receive few poems
And all poets.

Prayer to Persephone

Kore,
Who waits upon the end of me,
Lovely, regal, enthroned.

Kore,
Present at my next conception.

From Sunlight, down, and into darkness.

In darkness, Up,
and into light.

Hymn to Artemis

Artemis,
I honor you who surround the city
You who shall crack its walls and take it down.
I hear the sizzling beneath the concrete
The bursting buds, the mandibles.
Remember us when these streets are restored
To meadow
And when the beasts come to feed
Remember us who thought ourselves Forever
And masters of this World.
Forgive us our brutishness upon they we thought to long withhold.

May our meat be succulent to The Wild.

Hymn to Hermes

Hermes, who knows the ways
And who holds in keep the alchemies of the unspeakable.
Who whirls the Caduceus,
Transforms the silent into symbol
Then symbol into letters.

Yours, the recipe for the metals that hinge the gate.
You govern the number permitted to the secrets.
Admit me, Lord, into that number.
Open, then close, the gate.
Teach me where to step, though upon open space,
So to make my own way home.

2nd Hymn to Hermes

Hermes,
Who found the pieces of Dionysos.
Lend me the power to make whole the shattered vase.
Teach me to read the spaces in between
These fragments laid out across the desk
To imply the missing word.
Teach me to weight the contradictory,
Steering me always toward the highest.
Show me the straight line,
Let me hear the music amid the noise.
Let my Daimon coil, just a moment,
About the Caduceus.

Hermes,
Bearded and clean-shaven
Show me the numerals between one point six
And one point seven.
Let the strange syllables of strange tongues fall.
Teach my fingers to weight
The subtle tumblers in the lock
So that I, too,
Might swipe back a sinew of Zeus.

Hymn to Aphrodite

Aphrodite, Laughing,
Remind me that this world merits Joy.
Draw my eye to the violet petals
Sprung off that one lone flower in the alley.
Keep Despair away even while surrounded by Despair.
Keep my Soul clean, my Heart, light.

Tell me, then tell me again,
That the next world is all perfumed with love,
And that this world forever its image,
Though today is hard.
Aphrodite, let beauty never be far from me.

Office Prayer to Apollo

Apollo in whom we few work together,
One company.
Keep us as we each now go home.
Foster our reconvention come morning at morning's coffee.

Apollo, Seventh Night

Regard

the Mathematical perfection of the Waxing Quarter Moon,
the straight bisector slicing down
that swiftly, absolutely halves the Waxing Quarter Moon.
A single stroke of butter-knife, down.

And so tonight the perfect quietly pervades the real.
He is more, tonight, than intuition.
He is obvious. And everywhere.

Isis, Keep This Secret Hidden Tight

Isis, keep this secret hidden tight.
Even as the Moon is splashed with blood,
Set the regicide shall fall tonight.

Even though I hunger in this blight,
Arid moonscape blanches fertile mud.
Isis, keep this secret hidden tight.

Whisper softly underneath starlight.
Tap the dungeon walls in muffled code,
"Set the regicide shall fall tonight."

Broken, yet I know the hidden rite.
Broken, yet I know the stalk shall bud.
Isis, keep this secret hidden tight.

I have suffered in the people's plight.
Ate the seven asses put to stud.
Set the regicide must fall tonight.

Horus hatched is stretching wings for flight.
Horus save the land, restore the flood.
Isis, keep this secret hidden tight.
Set the regicide shall fall tonight.

Two Hymns to Zeus

I.
Zeus, who sees the Cosmos Whole.
Zeus, who sees the trillion faces of the generations.
See me.
You who know best that I am not alone,
Guide my step to shelter for the night.
Find those behind closed doors
Who hold you open in their hearts.

II.
Zeus, keep my duty clear.
May I ever be a comfort
To those straddled by misfortune
Without regard for whether this one
Suffered a bad turn at Tyche's wheel,
Or that one suffered hate scratched on a lead sheet,
Or even the quick just strike your thunderbolt.
Judgment is yours.
Service, mine.
This is my portion, to answer the door,
To offer my pitcher to those who thirst.

Poly Theos

They,
that consist the fine plasmas
then dis-whisper subatomic and into mind sublime.

Theirs,
the first
and therein strongest hands,
the fingers prerequisite
to mine.

Iron Fits Ogun

Iron fits Ogun.
He is patient, as is this iron
That has sat through Sun and wind and rain.
Upon Ogun the raindrops ping.
Rusted weights half-hid in dandelions,
Once some little motor part,
Once this drove some fit machine.

Ogun, who waits inside the mountain.
Ogun, the stuff of fired nails.

Within this six inch cloud of risen dust
Ogun that bottom quarter-inch
Whose grains, red-brown and massive
Only just bounce up off the earth, once,
Then scarcely roll.

Ogun your praises shake the atoms in my acid chain.
Ogun you give my blood its aftertaste.

Ogun 2

Ogun, I relish this green moment
When the memories between us are few.
Something about the Nok,
Who straightaway grew from stone to iron,
Who came before Yoruba and Benin.

I think when these peoples rose up
You were there, Ogun,
Waiting.
Now you wait for me.

Ogun,
Between us the absolute of old blood,
The red that flows beneath your gaze

That exudes magnetic fields
That pinch the stone banks inward
And squeeze
And raise the pressure.
I think you wait for me.

Four Sips, Demeter

My chili doesn't rot so quick anymore,
Only at the slow pace of lentil not
the same-day despoilage of flesh left out.
Two bourbons sit beside the bowl, one mine the other, Hers.
Haven't tasted bourbon in fifteen years, but it seems right for this,
Kitchen-witch instincts working double.
I'm about to be bad to my liver for a while.

Outside the window above the railing,
Two palm leaves dangle down.
I offhand decide their texture matches that of corn husks,
Sip,
And so begins the journey.

Out the window I take wing to an Iowa of my imaginized memory
Of a longago overnight roadside stay.
I dysremember the gentle rollingness of the hallucinatory hills,
Their game of peekaboo with the horizon.
I dysremember the infinity of the corn.

I recline on cornstalks, one bourbon in hand,
piglet wriggling happy tucked close in my free arm,
Not big enough yet to be hard to hold but
Eager, squirmy enough that the ice-cubes swirl inside the glass.
Forward-facing spinning hooves try the air,

Back-kick clips two buttons off my shirt.
Pig hooves sharper in my ribs than my ribs expected.
On my belt one knife, sheathed.
Your work, to remain so.

Now up high a Canadian and and an Eastern front collide.
The corntips sway all together,
All across the rolling hills as far as sight,
One broad breeze wall stirs the corn entire.
Demeter's breath blows sweet across the fields.
She bends the corn as one.
She whistles between the stalks
As into the two cups of my ears.
She cools the piglet in my arm's embrace,
She chills our bourbon beyond the ice.
Lady, I propose a mystery.
Sip.
Piglet limp, becalmed.
Friend.
Another Moon I'd have loved you roasted.

Ready to run?
Piglet goes yeh yeh yeh.
Then this belted knife my witness
I release you from the burden of my appetites.
And let go.

You hit ground hooves spinning, and gone,
A heartbeat then the corntips jump in a beeline, out, and gone,
The receding snapping of the stalks, out, and silence.
You will find the water.
Grow fat on the fat parts of the corn,
And so grow old.
Curl two great and terrifying tusks

And run forever.
This mystery doesn't need your dying.

Again, the whole field stirs.
Broad waves impress into the corn,
The whole field softly lashed by wave after
Hieroglyphic wave bestroke the corn.

She bothers up waves across the waters,
She buffets the airborne flocks,
She blasts the tips of the corn.
She before whom all sit one table.
Demeter whispers first the horizontal power.

If this form, then let this form grow strong.
Let this body take up the upright posture of the stalks,
That weather all but the locust, the machete, and the torch.
Let us see what strong decades might yet be wrung
From this body only just turned overripe,
Then only afterward commit to the Daughter beneath the grass.
Sip.

If this tongue then let this tongue be delighted.
Savor the white sauce bubbled out
From cracks in the croquette's browned crust,
Stir-fry the sprouts in olive till crisp,
Singed at the outermost leaves,
Shell the walnuts, bowl the walnuts,
Blend in one ginger slice with the kale and the avocado,
Discern the cumin from the curry,
Learn new ways to butter and to cheese,
When one pinch of marjoram and when two,

Which days to chop slow cook and which to dine raw, on
One whole watermelon and a pack of almonds,
And befriend the creatures of this Cosmos.

Here, then, to higher pleasures.
Sip.

Now the bottom of the bourbon I commit to the soil of the corn,
to the Mother, here, to the Daughter, below, and there, two buttons,
Cleaned by the bourbon splash of the soil of the corn.
I bend and scoop them up, to carry off as coin,
Return.

Two palm leaves sway green outside my window.
Above a red steel railing. Hear.
It shudders of an unseen power.

Hymn to Ares

Ares the engorged,
Ares veined,
Ares the god that wants.

Ares the lit sulfur,
red beet red god
and the hunger, needle-bright,
five days gone unfed.

Ares the pounder on the walls.
Ares who must get in.

Odysseus' AfterWords

Darling Circe, leading me to sin.
As I rest my head between your thighs
Whisper me what beast I would've been.

Ichor pulses cool beneath your skin.
By this deathless blood you mesmerize.
Darling Circe, leading me to sin.

Turning sailors into Otherkin.
Some to ursinate, some leonize.
Whisper me what beast I would've been.

Kiss you up and down your eight foot ten.
Let's again before this morning dries.
Darling Circe, leading me to sin.

Would my sweat bead up a dorsal fin?
Does my tongue inspire butterflies?
Whisper me what beast I would've been.

Now again to taste the light within,
Stir your repertoire of little cries.
Darling Circe, leading me to sin.
Whisper me what beast I would've been.

Dawn Devotion, Apollo

Apollo the refining seam inside the common,
Morning's triple blade impressed,
My lip my cheek my throat
Straight mini snow plow lanes in white lather,
A new menthol underscent unspools into the frankincensed rooms.

My face my scalp, splash! two hands bowled with cold shower water
The beading of the cold shower water
Splash! and slick the blue tiles
The beading of the cold shower water
White lather incinnamoned with hair clips whirling down the pipe
Into the city.

I am clean, and ready for the city.

Acknowledgements

"Odysseus' AfterWords" was published in *Circe's Cauldron: Tales of Magic and Witchcraft*. Bibliotheca Alexandrina and *The Road Not Taken: A Journal For Formal Verse*.

"Villanelle to the Goddess Hekate" was published in *Circe's Cauldron: Pagan Poems and Tales of Magic and Witchcraft*. Biblioteca Alexandrina.

"Urban's Noir" was published in *ActiveMuse*.

"Let Us Turn Aside This Blackened Bread" was published by *The Night Forest Cell of Radical Poetry*.

"Evanescent Are the Saffron Veils" was collected in The Keys to the Kingdom: Unlocking the Forms, by *The Poetry Kingdom*.

My poems have also appeared in *Snakeskin Poetry Webzine*, *Gods & Radicals Press*, and elsewhere. I maintain **Todd Jackson Poetry on YouTube**, where these and other poems are regularly published in video form.

I received my BA in English from Clarion University of Pennsylvania and my MA in English from Johns Hopkins University.

"Todd Jackson Poetry" logo by Laura Zollar. The cover image, from my sketches, photo-edited by Eric Jackson